S.A.F.E

Corey Phinney

All rights reserved. No part of this book can be reproduced, used, stored, transmitted or displayed in any form, or by any means (electronic, mechanical, or otherwise) now or hereafter devised – including photocopy, recording or any information storage and retrieval system along with any quotes and or pictures used in this book. Please do not participate in or encourage piracy of copyrighted materials in violation of the author's rights. Purchase only authorized editions.

Published by: Corey Phinney

Copyright © 2014 Corey Phinney

ISBN-13: 978-1492283904
Title ID: 4421808

S.A.F.E. Written by Author © Corey Phinney
www.coreyphinney77.blogspot.com

Poetry by: Author © Matthew Ganem
www.mattganemthepoet.com

Poetry by Author: © Keith Laporta
www.facebook.com/keithylaportapoet

Printed & Published in the United States of America

Revised Copy and re-edited by: Nicole Penticost on October 20th, 2014

Dedication

This book is in memory of all our loved ones lost to drug addiction and in strength of those in recovery.

In Memory of

Shaun Alan Flynn
10/7/77 – 9/28/12

I don't want to see anymore of our loved ones on memorial cards because of addiction. We must lock up the dealers and get addicts the help that is needed. These are people that need help. Enough hearing there's not enough beds available or we don't take your insurance. Enough is enough.
~ Corey Phinney

Contents

1- S.A.F.E — 1

2- Introduction — 3

3- Understanding the Addict (There People too) — 4

4- An Addicts Story — 9

5- © Matthew Ganem - Poet — 12

6- © Keith Laporta – Poet — 19

7- Statistics & Facts — 27

8- Diseases — 30

9- Awareness & Education — 38

10- Recovery & Detox — 40

11- Finding Resources — 44

12- Emotions and Healing — 45

13- Stress, Worrying, Anxiety — 47

14- Addiction & Living Sober — 48

Remembrance — 51
Strength & Recovery — 56
The S.A.F.E. Project's Affiliated Site — 57
Recommended sites to join — 58
The S.A.F.E. Project Pledge — 59
Journal — 61
Special Thanks — 63

1 - S.A.F.E.

The S.A.F.E. project is about helping others; we are here to tell you that you're not alone and that other people are going through what you're going through. S.A.F.E. is about education, creating hope, awareness and change surrounding the drug epidemic that we're facing in the United States. The S.A.F.E. project holds addiction awareness events such as rally's, celebration of recovery, vigils and walks to promote addiction awareness, while remembering our loved ones in hopes that someday we can create after rehab recovery programs so once he or she is released from rehab and/or prison they can continue their rehabilitation with meetings, indoor and outdoor activities, workshops, and so much more. To help them have a place to feel SAFE and to get help without the pressures of worry. To help find a job, housing and continue their education, we will always be there for YOU during and after the process toward sobriety. We have started a NEW program called Adopt an Addict. We find sober and valid driver licensed people to give rides to and from meetings, court, shopping and maybe even a place to stay temporarily, pending on circumstances. This program which has just launched in 2014 has been doing very well and this is just one step closer to our goal of our after rehab long-term program. Thank you again to all who volunteer for us. This book is full of informational tools to help detect and help those who suffer from addiction.

The S.A.F.E. project currently works with addiction, single parents and all sorts of other charities and foundations, locally and all around the United States. For more information on what we do, e-mail us at: TheSAFEproject77@yahoo.com

2 - Introduction

Corey Phinney is worldly known for his inspirational award – winning blog and social networking in which he inspires others with his upbeat daily quotes and positive writing with his outlook on life. Corey uses his gift of connecting with others toward helping others while doing his own self work. His kind hearted, tough love and belief in others has helped him pay it forward again and again and has helped others pay it forward as well. Corey has never been an addict, but that doesn't mean he doesn't understand addiction; Corey has helped thousands of people and has also taken some great personal losses with close friends. Corey is very well known for all he does with addiction awareness and volunteering. Corey inspires so many people and welcomes everyone he comes in contact with into his life. Corey is the founder of The S.A.F.E. project along with many other projects going on at once, this book is one of many. When you purchased this book, you just helped someone; so for that alone, Corey is very grateful and thankful.

~ Introduction Written by Anonymous Fan

3 - Understanding the Addict
(There People too)

The person you once knew may have lost their way into the world of addiction and you have to now find who that person now is, not who they were and that starts with understanding the addict and the addiction. Everyone has a story of how they started. It could've been an accident or a doctor that kept refilling a script. Could've been so many things, but now you have to face and understand the addiction, this persons self worth, and all they could and can be. Understand what they're going through isn't an easy road and it could be lifelong recovery. Many people do not understand why or how other people become addicted to drugs. It's often mistakenly assumed that drug abusers lack moral principles or will power and that they could stop using drugs simply by choosing to change their behavior. In reality, drug addiction is a complex disease, and quitting takes more than good intentions or a strong will. In fact, because drugs change the brain in ways that foster compulsive drug abuse, quitting is difficult, even for those who are ready and willing to do so. We know more about how drugs work in the brain than ever before, and we also know that drug addiction can be successfully treated to help people stop abusing drugs and lead productive lives.

Prevention is the key

The S.A.F.E. project believes drug addiction is a preventable disease. Results from research have shown that prevention programs involving families, schools, communities, and the media are effective in reducing drug abuse. Although many events and cultural factors affect drug abuse trends, when youths perceive drug abuse as harmful, they reduce their drug taking. Thus, education and outreach are key in helping youth and people of all ages; this is why The S.A.F.E. project spreads Addiction Awareness across the United States so YOU will understand the risks of drug abuse. Teachers, parents, medical and public health professionals must keep sending the message that drug addiction can be prevented if one never abuses drugs and we are open with our youth about drugs and the addictiveness that occurs.

The S.A.F.E. project Recommends
- Journal
- Circle Groups
- Online Communities
- Local Recovery Centers
- Staying Active
  So many wonderful resources out there you just have to look and ask questions.

A journal is a good way to document your thoughts and have the freedom of writing what you feel without judgment; examples would be hopes, dreams, and goals. What do you want to achieve? You can virtually write down anything from what you love about your life to what you hate. I recommend setting a clock for 60 minutes and just write everything that comes to your mind and re-read it in a couple days. Make a check-list of some of the things you want to accomplish, what fears you want to face and put it somewhere that you will see it every day and check it off as you complete them and add as you check. This isn't magic but it's a great solution and does work for addicts and non-addicts.

Circle Groups are great, usually small and intimate and gives you a voice. I hold a lot of online and outdoor circle groups, mine aren't just about addiction or grieving but always open conversations about anything, I'm not a licensed sociologist but you don't have to be one to listen to people and it's a great way to meet new life-long friends. I would recommend you try one out if you haven't already.

Online Communities are also a wonderful platform, I will have all the ones I am affiliated with toward the end of the book and will list some I recommend.

Local Recovery Centers, I know a lot of people hear no beds available or don't take your insurance but local recovery centers are suppose to be there for help, so go ask questions, see what support groups they have, and maybe find long term placement for someone. Get information, do a lot of research and keep calling every day.

<u>Staying Active</u> – Go for a run, hike or swim. Join a gym, try something new and exciting. This works for addicts and non-addicts, keep busy! Try anything that interests you. This is a worldwide epidemic and we need to educate ourselves so we can educate others. It starts with understanding the addict. You may be reading this as an addict or a non-addict or someone in recovery, but you only get out of recovery what you put into it, just like life; what you put in you will get in return so keep yourself busy and stay with a program; like NA or AA whatever works best for you.

"Everything in life happens for a reason and comes to us in the form of opportunity, when you know better you do better, don't look at this as a setback but as an opportunity to do something bigger then you thought you could do.
~ Corey Phinney

"These people were somebody before they became part of this awful epidemic, a cheerleader, football player, traveler, movie buff, it isn't just the poor getting high, but even celebrity's . Everyone needs someone and just note you are not alone."
~ Corey Phinney

"If I could take all of the pain and stress away, I would, but I can't and I know the strength within, happens from the strength of others"
~ Corey Phinney

4 - An Addicts Story

A young guy we will call Brock for the sake of the story; prior to drugs was very popular and very into sports. He had a house, a good job, a couple of cars, a fiancé who loved him, a child who adored him, and lots of family and friends. An injury would be the start of a bad roller coaster ride and would change his life forever. It was a hot end of the summer's day and the end of a baseball league he was playing on. After an epic win for his team and amazing time with his teammates, it was time for everyone to say their goodbyes until next season. Brock was driving home from the game when another car went through a red light and smashed the driver side of Brocks door, slamming his head off the driver's side window, and then slamming his face off the steering wheel dislocating his jaw, breaking his wrist and bruises all over his face and arms from the impact. Brock would get rushed to the hospital from all of his injuries. Brocks Fiancé and family would soon rush to the hospital to be at his bedside. Brock would find only having to wear a jaw guard for a few weeks, from the impact of the crash he would have some back pains, damaged wrist and jaw dislocated, so the doctor prescribed him Percocet because the pain was so unbearable but instead of prescribing a few at a time, Brock was receiving them on a monthly basis for about a year or so. The doctor would finally shut Brock off at one of his scheduled doctor visits; cold turkey, not weaning him off or prior warning and by then it was too late. He was already addicted. This would eventually lead to purchasing Percocet 30's, street value is about $30.00 a pill. So after not working for awhile and spending almost all of his savings on these pills, he would first lose his fiancé and child then the loss of his house, cars and everything he worked so hard for. Brock didn't see himself as an addict; all he saw was the doctor just shut him off and complained all the time his entire dynamic on life had changed and everyone saw it but him. After losing his Fiancé he decided to try heroin and we all know you can't just try it, statistics show once you try it once you are hooked. Brock would later move back home with his parents. After stealing, lying and getting arrested a few times, Brocks family decided to toss him out, so Brock would end up on the streets and in and out of jail and rehabs while still doing drugs. Brock's addiction started with pills and ended with heroin. Brock is the success story after years of doing drugs, a few overdoses, and in and out of court he finally started the road of recovery. It would be the loss of a good friend of an overdose that would re-change and direct his life. He didn't want to go that way, so he started focusing on recovery and slowly starting to see his son like he didn't before, apologizing to everyone who endured his pain for years. Brock today is an advocate for awareness and very involved with The S.A.F.E. project. He just wants you all to know that recovery is real and sometimes you have to lose all the things you want and love to realize you have a problem. Brock has buried many friends since his recovery, but he has also saved just as many. Brock goes to meetings daily and is slowly working on his relationships. If you can get anything from his story it would be; one beautiful afternoon with friends ended with losing everything basically overnight. Brock has learned values from this awful experience; he re-evaluated his life and found what truly is important in his life now and that's his sobriety, son, family and his new circle of friends.

How do you say no to heroin?

I know a lot of people may think that the inhaled form of heroin is less dangerous to use then injecting it. I think many people are just not aware of the devastating toll heroin, in any form has on another person's life and everyone involved. If anyone offers you heroin just say "NO" and walk away. Heroin is not worth the long-term damage it does to your body and could also lead to death and/or lifetime of recovery.

5 - © Matthew Ganem - Poet

My name is Matt Ganem, I'm the father to a handsome son and beautiful daughter and a recovering heroin addict. I've been clean since April 21, 2006 and I'm also the author of The Shadow of an Addict. I put my story out there so people know that you can overcome this and live a normal life and that addiction can touch anybody; it doesn't matter your social class, skin color, or sexual preference. It affects all walks of life. There are a lot of good people that fall into the grips of drug addiction. A couple of bad choices or hanging around the wrong people and you can quickly spiral out of control. I'm lucky to still be here because most of us don't make it out alive and it's for that reason I scream out my story for the world to hear it hoping that I give others strength, hope and something they can relate to through my written words.

Repeat After Me
When its hard trying to make it through the day
Just know eventually the sun shines through the rain
Instead of facing the problem you'd rather run away
Using a chemical to disguise the shame
Filling inside your vein
You'd rather die than change
So you get higher than a plane
Just trying to maintain
Chaos becomes normal
Using that drug like a portal
That has you feeling immortal
Savoring every morsel
Pick your chin up kid
Before that needle leaves you dead or doing a bid
Scoring dope and coke you feel like your doing it big
This is no way to live
I see you hitting detox
Talking the talk
Only to have your feet touch the block
And you're already desperate for another shot
Or think you can smoke a crack rock
But addiction is more cunning than a fox
It tricks you into thinking you alright
Cause lighting a pipe was never your vice
So you inhale paradise
Reactivating the parasite
Now you need landing gear
Cause your chest is beating out to here

Paranoia has you peeking out the window in fear
You don't know who might be out there

On hands and knees combing through carpet hairs
You're full of despair

Dialing Carlos, Bapi, Juan or Jose
Whatever fake name they gave you to say
Please bring me a bag of dope to save the day
So you sit on the corner and wait
"5 minutes Papi" but you know they're gonna be late
Dealing with the shakes
Sweat dripping down your face
And your whole body aches
Knowing that bag of dope is gonna make you feel great
But what if you take to much
Addicts are overcome by lust
Addicted to the rush
Feels better than when you bust
And its never enough
You can't escape the grip
Selling your soul for a filled syringe
Sinking in the tip
Then drift
To where the problems don't mean shit
You nod out to the point it looks like your sucking your own dick
Listen, I don't know why the earth spins
But one things for certain
If you keep getting high it'll be closed curtains
Death is always lurking
To make you another forgotten person

Here's a secret on what's not working
Shooting up to escape the lows
Will only bury you in a hole

Next time you try to get clean refuse to fold
Before your found in a bathroom blue and cold
You might lose your soul

And I don't want you to go
Believe in yourself
Swallow your pride and ask for some help

I don't want your memorial card added to the ones on the shelf
It only takes one time for the final blow to be dealt
This shits bad for your health
The world is a beautiful place if you only open your eyes
Hold your head to the sky
And stop getting high
Just give getting clean a try
Nobody wants to see you die
I was lucky to survive
And I'm more than happy to be alive
Repeat after me if you can do it so can I
You gave birth to my emptiness
Depriving me of the one thing that I needed
You and it was effortless
Flipping through text messages
But I deleted everything that reminded me
Of you I still taste your bitter sweet misery

Forgotten in the black hole of yesterday
Light disappears inside of dark memories
Oh sweet misery
When it was you and I
I knew I could be your guy

First moments brought clear skies
No fear of goodbyes
I barely had to try
Now its suicide
My broken heart inside
Beats ready to die
Thump thump thump
Love is a strange thing

For you
I would have done anything
Gave you a wedding ring
Put a pistol to the head of a king

And run him for everything
Never expected the pain your love would bring
Curled up on the ground
Break me down
Wishing you would come back around
Maybe rekindle that first feeling that we found
But I'm alone now
Staring at a stranger
Who are you?
And what did you do with my reflection
A thousand other question
Were deflected by my depression
I was always told to count my blessings

But my sickness heals from your medicine
I'm under the weather but I keep telling myself don't let her in
Never ever ever again
Touching the marks you left on my skin
Remembering how it feels within

When we made love it was like a piece of heavens light
But your love is like a pack of rabid mice
Eating at away at my life
It seems like I'll never be alright
Dreaming about you when I'm laying at night
You used to look so beautiful in the moonlight
Doing everything I can
Just to hold you in my hands
But you wouldn't understand
I chased you

You never had to chase me
I'll always run back to you
You will always be my first baby
My first lady
My first love

I never put anyone else above
Not friends, not blood
It was us
You satisfied me but I was never good enough
Attached to your ball and chain I was cuffed up
The bubble guts before we touched
There was something about you that made me erupt
Made me corrupt

Lust
It must have been
But me and you are still brought up in discussion
Even the thought of you has my blood pumping
Its disgusting
To a point that its hard to function
You crippled my soul
That more than tripled your hold

I watch the ripples go
In a simple flow
I didn't fall in love with you, I fell in love with how you made me feel
When we were together I made you my shield
I fell in love with the fact that I didn't have to deal
I'm just mad at myself for falling for something that wasn't real
How can you love something that will never love you back
There's nothing harder than that
I still have your scars from the past
That turned my heart into shards of glass

Scattered across the tracks
On the part of the path
That wants me to be brought back
Relapse
Ice running through my veins
Still asking for your name

I just hope you loved me the same
Until I got rid of the shame
You took a piece of me with you
But that's what x-lovers do
Still being here is a miracle
After everything my beautiful Lady Heroin put me through

6 - © Keith Laporta - Poet

My name's Keith Laporta. I'm a recovering heroin addict that's been sober for some time now. I'm also a poet that writes about my struggles with addiction, what I went through and how I got clean. I'm 27 years old and grew up during a drug epidemic like today; only today it's much worse. I've lost many friends due to suicides and drug overdoses, so today I write my poetry to touch the hearts and lives of those still struggling with addiction, I write to save lives....

Do you know what it's like being raised in a broken home
when your dad's dead and your people go out and leave you home alone?

At 8 years old fending for your own
Well this is the life that I've known
A house full of dope fiends and crack heads
In the other room I can smell the crack smoke from my bed
I watched my mother struggle with drugs
But I didn't know what it was cause I was young
I was born with crack smoke in my lungs
A newborn baby strung

Born to a life of addiction

A life of heart ache and prison
With no food in the kitchen
I was the youngest of four siblings
My brothers were nodding out all the time

But I didn't know it was cause they were getting high
I was a kid and didn't know nothing about life

But growing up I destroyed mine
I didn't have discipline and rules to live by
I did my own thing
No one Cared about the trouble I was getting in
Or when I started using oxys and heroin
I never even made it to high school
I went to Foster homes and dys too
Only if people knew the shit that I've been through
And what it's like to walk in my shoes
It wasn't easy growing up being me
I barely have any good memories
I only know my dad by a headstone in a cemetery
I was infected by addiction genetically
I was cursed with a life of bad luck
Like a broken mirror that lightning struck
Fuck
Another young victim born to drugs
A distorted family tree
Bare branches with no leaves
Except for this junkie
Who lived through hell to get clean
A family of addicts

Living through a syringe filled with magic
My life was fucking tragic
It's like bad luck is everlasting
My whole life I been battling this disease

Trying to get on my feet
But it's hard to make ends meet
Standing in the shadow of the beast

So before you judge me and my poetry
Come face to face with me and judge me openly
Try on my shoes and see if you can live my life socially

After growing up in this world soullessly
Shooting heroin uncontrollably
I literally lived the life that I bleed across these lines
no exaggeration no lies
Due to my drug use I even tried committing suicide
I was brought up in a broken home full of crime
And I did mine and served the time
I still feel as though I'm still kid inside
But there's always time for change
That's why I'm still standing here today
Without injecting poison in my veins
Writing poetry to pave a new way
Creating a legacy
For you people to remember me

Thoughts of a junkie

I can't get this needle outta my hand

It's glued there
I'm a broken man
Been numbing these feelings for the majority of my life span

Heroin full spoon on the table
Thoughts of an addict transforming into an angel
You'd only understand if this disease plagues you

Wishing you could reach out for someone to save you

Uncap the syringe
Add the cotton
And suck up the heroin
Find the vein and stick the pin in

Push in the plug
And fall in love
Once again with a beautiful rush
A feeling that takes the breath outta your lungs
Oh how I love these drugs

But I hate how they destroy my life
How they make me lie
And hurt every one that stood by my side
And make my family cry

I gotta get outta this cage
And quit sticking needles in my veins
I need to find a way

Too put out these demons flames
I gotta find my will to change

This shit is killing my friends
For all I know I could be next
The next addict on his death bed
How long of my life do I have left

Why do I continue to use you
After all that you put me through

Why do I continue
To keep shooting you

I'm staring at you in my spoon
Looking right through you
Thinking about the shit you make me do
And the shit you put me through
That's when I get mad and say I'm done with you

I take one more look at you
And finally tip over the spoon....

AN ADDICTS SUICIDE LETTER

red and blue sirens going off in my mind
crowd of spectators off to the side
cops looking around for evidence to find
only to turn a blind eye
cause they realized
it was only an addicts suicide

emts bring the body out on a stretcher
a young addicts soul gone forever
heart poured out in the suicide letter
how this kid didn't have the courage to surrender

the kid was sick of chasing the drugs
feeling the guilt from hurting the people he loved
he was going crazy from the angel dust

keeping his drug use on the hush
making crack pipes out of cans of orange crush
fell in love with the cocaine rush

friends drifted away as they see him struggle
neighbors saying the kid is nothing but trouble
kicked out on the streets he was forced to hustle
sleeping in an abandoned buildings rubble

*wrapping himself in a welcome mat
the tears flow as he thinks of mom and dad
he just wants to go back
but his parents don't wanna hear that
they just wanna let a few nights pass
having their son sleep with the rats*

*letting all types of emotions flow
this addict just wanted to let go
so before he filled the syringe with of dope
he wrote a letter to let his family know
and this is the letter that he wrote*

*"mom and dad I'm sorry I was a bad son
I'm sorry for all that I've done
I'm not doing this to hurt you
its just all that I'm going through
I'm sorry that this is how I'm saying good bye
I'm really gonna miss you guys*

*its just I couldn't get rid of these demons inside
I cant stop getting high
mom and dad don't worry I'll be alright please don't cry
I love you I'll be looking down on you from the sky*

goodbye"......

*so he ties off and sticks the needle in
pushes the plunge filling his veins with heroin
killing himself within
a young addict overdosing
that couldn't win
his battle with addiction......*

*I'm the furthest thing from perfect
But when I write my poetry it has a purpose
I'm a non-profit merchant
I just volunteer my service
Because I know how this disease can be a burden
I know I'm clean, but I still fight every day
I fight back with dismay
I have no time to play
The beast has been in his cage so long he's beginning to decay
But I still got a few demons to slay
Feels like I walked through a portal from a dark dimension
I'm holding off the progression*

*The evil That the addiction is intending
I'm still mending
Back together my life that's been shredded
I'm picking up the pieces of my past
I finally have these demons trapped*

*I'm ready to attack
I'm moving forward and I'm not looking back
I've been through too much to do that
I'm just glad that I can have an impact
On others before they relapse
Too many of us are dying*

*I don't wanna see anymore angels flying
Families crying
It's hard to make a difference in this world but I'm trying
Because I'm sick of seeing these overdoses*

multiplying
I dedicate my poetry to save lives
To those contemplating suicide
And to those that think they can't stop getting high
Cause I know what it feels like
They say that the eyes are the Windows to the soul
So take a look in mine and you'll see that you're not alone
I'll hand you a ladder to climb outta that hole
As long as you hold on and don't let go
You can make it out of that slump
And have those monsters trumped
Have them crushed

Help others and be glad on how many lives you've touched
Look back and think why you succumbed to drugs
Just keep doing you and never give up
Keep fighting cause addiction doesn't have a cure
Just build a network and keep it secure
Keep your heart pure
And I promise you will succeed And that I'm sure
And you won't have to worry no more..

7 - Statistics & Facts

There are over 1.2 million "occasional" heroin users in the United States and over 200,000 people who could be classified as addicted to the drug.

The average heroin addict ingests between 150mg and 250mg of the drug per day.

Heroin overdoses have caused more deaths than traffic accidents in the past several years.

There are believed to be at least 700,000 people in the United States who need heroin addiction treatment but are not receiving it.

Heroin is made from the white, milky liquid exuded from the opium poppy; heroin is a powerful and dangerous drug which is often injected directly into the bloodstream with a needle. When injected, heroin reaches the brain in just 7 or 8 seconds. Using heroin for even a short time can create physical and psychological dependence. In large doses, heroin can cause breathing to become shallow or to stop all together.

The physical and mental addiction to heroin is a difficult one to break, even when it is destroying the user's health and life. The intense craving for heroin can be both physical and mental. For the user, it becomes a way of life. Every day centers on getting and using heroin. After continued use, more heroin is needed to achieve the same effects. This results in a very costly habit. Once addicted, a user must have heroin every 8 to 12 hours. Withdrawal symptoms include fevers, chills, nausea, aching, diarrhea and muscle spasms; most symptoms last 3 to 5 days.

The Physical Risk

- Sleepiness
- Skin sores / abscesses
- Slow breathing
- Collapsed veins
- Loss of appetite
- Heart damage
- Constipation
- Pregnant users may risk still birth, miscarriage
- Loss of sexual desire
- Malnutrition
- Severe bleeding
- AIDS (through shared needles)
- Anemia

- Death by overdose

Social Risk
- Family life suffers
- School performance and work performance declines
- Dependency may cause neglect of other important needs

Mental Health and Behavior Risk
- Extreme mood swings
- Poor concentration
- Depression
- Secretive behavior

Legal Risk

Unlike some similar drugs, heroin is considered too dangerous even for medical use. Using or selling heroin is against the law. Offenders usually go to jail.

8 - Diseases

The diseases of concern to heroin users:

Hepatitis

You can get hepatitis from ingesting heroin in any way but it is most likely with snorting because the heroin is never cooked. Hepatitis has a strong association with injection because of unhygienic procedures. Regardless of the method of administration, when you keep the company of heroin users, you risk infection of hepatitis. Although it may not seem the case, a sneeze or a cough can propel particles ten or more feet from the location of the ejection. These particles can land on syringes or other implements thereby being input into your body. Hepatitis is the inflammation of the liver. There are several different forms of this disease but three are primary: A, B, and C. Each is caused by a distinct virus. I will discuss each form of hepatitis below but first we must discuss the liver and its importance to life. The liver is a regenerative organ. It has three primary functions: modulation of blood sugar (energy) levels, creation of bile, and removal of poisons. The liver gets blood from two sources: oxygenated blood from the hepatic artery and nutrient rich blood from the portal vein which comes from the stomach, intestines, spleen, and pancreas. The blood from the small intestines carries absorbed nutrients such as sugars and amino acids. When there is an excess of these nutrients, the liver stores them. When there is a deficiency, the liver releases them. In this way, the liver buffers the blood sugar levels so that they never get too high nor too low. The liver also secretes bile. Bile is the substance in the body that digests fat down to sugar so that the body can use it. Probably the most important function of the liver is removing poisons from the body. This is critical to the body's ability to heal itself. Most drugs are seen by the liver as poisons, so excessive drug use can greatly tax the liver. Alcohol is particularly associated with liver damage. In fact, alcohol abuse is the number one cause of cirrhosis of the liver. Cirrhosis of the liver is the chronic destruction of its cells. A cirrhotic liver loses its organization which is critical to this complex organ. As a result of this, the liver stops functioning. When the liver cells are damaged, they are replaced by scar tissue. This tissue has none of the liver cell functions. In effect, that part of the liver is no longer liver. When cirrhosis of the liver begins, it causes the liver to be enlarged because of the regenerative process that is happening. But later the liver shrinks because of the contraction of the scar tissue.

Hepatitis A is the least serious form of hepatitis. It usually comes from contaminated water or food and spreads under conditions of poor sanitation. The incubation period is two to six weeks. Its symptoms include: loss of appetite, nausea, mild fever, darkness of urine, and sometimes jaundice (yellowish pigmentation of the skin). In general, the liver will be enlarged but no permanent liver damage results.

Hepatitis B is much more serious than type A. It can lead to chronic (long-term) hepatitis or cirrhosis of the liver. Hepatitis B is generally transmitted via blood: shared or dirty syringes and unprotected sex. The symptoms for type A are about the same as for type B but the onset is slower: it generally takes two to six months for type A symptoms to appear. The severity of the disease depends largely on the physical health of the sufferer before the disease took effect. This is why Hepatitis can be particularly hard on addicts.

Hepatitis C is quite similar to type B. There are only a few differences. The incubation period is highly variable. Generally it is anywhere from two weeks to six months. But increasingly the disease seems able to stay dormant many years. There is currently no cure for Hepatitis C.

AIDS

As if anyone doesn't know this: AIDS is an acronym for Acquired Immunodeficiency Syndrome and it is believed to be caused by HIV which is another acronym of Human Immunodeficiency Virus. AIDS destroys your immune system. This makes you very susceptible to infection. This is because HIV invades your white blood cells and destroys their ability to fight infection. HIV is a retrovirus which means that it carries its genetic information via RNA instead of DNA. What does this mean? Nothing. Nothing at all. What matters is this: if you get AIDS you will die within about a decade. Once infected with HIV, it will lay dormant for two to eight years. Once symptoms develop you are said to have AIDS. These symptoms are: weight loss, enlarged lymph nodes, diarrhea, fever, and night sweats. If you experience any of the symptoms of AIDS you should, of course, see a doctor. But generally, a doctor will not be able to do much for you if it is caught after becoming full blown AIDS. For this reason, you should get tested for HIV infection as often as is reasonable. This means every six months if you are involved in dangerous activities such as sharing needles or having unprotected sex. If you are living a reasonably clean life then you should test for HIV every two years. If you're doing heroin, you aren't living that clean of a life. Various drugs and therapies can prolong the life of a person infected with HIV. But by far the best thing you can do for yourself is to get healthy. Your first reaction to finding out you are infected will likely be to submerge yourself in heroin, but this will only put added pressure on your body and cause you to have a shorter, and more important, sicker life. Try to look on the bright side: you might live longer with AIDS alone than you would have with heroin alone.

Leukoencephalopath

Leukoencephalopathy is a neurological disease that adversely affects the material that surrounds neurons in the brain and spinal cord--helping them transmit messages and protecting them from electrical activity from other neurons. It was first noted in the 1930s in children suffering from leukemia. The first case associated with heroin use was documented in 1982. The symptoms of the disease include mental deterioration, vision loss, speech difficulty, loss of coordination, paralysis, and, ultimately, coma and even death in as many as 25% of those with the disease. The most common way that heroin users get this disease is by infection when the immune system is weak due to AIDS. A relatively small number of people contract the disease directly as a result of smoking heroin. The mechanism is still not understood, but it is believed to result from contact with an uncommon adulterant used to **cut** street heroin. The earliest symptoms of leukoencephalopathy are slurred speech and difficulty walking. Any heroin smoker showing these signs (which may come on many days after the last use), should see a doctor immediately. If treated quickly recovery is possible.

Endocarditis

Endocarditis is an infection of the inner lining of the heart. If left untreated, it is fatal. There are two disease types: Acute Infectious Endocarditis and Subacute Infectious Endocarditis. They are caused by different strains of bacteria and progress at different rates. The subacute form is most common. It is caused by a Streptoccus bacterium (the same thing that causes Strep Throat) called *Streptoccus viridans*. If untreated it will kill you within a year. The acute form of Endocarditis is caused by a couple of different bacteria: *Staphylococcus aureus* and *Streptococcus hemolyticus*. It will kill you in about a month. The bacteria adhere to the inner lining of the heart--the endocardium. Once there, they grow. These bacterial colonies become very large and pieces of them break off and enter the circulatory system. These bacterial "particles" then get trapped in various places in the body. Because of this, you will have some indication that you should see a doctor. The symptoms are: Petechiae in the skin, blood in the urine, and a long-term low-grade fever.

Pulmonary Edema

Pulmonary Edema is the swelling of lung tissue. The main result of this is to reduce the lung capacity, usually to about 50% of its full capacity. It can lead to very potent pneumonia which can lead to death. Generally this is a problem associated with heroin related **sudden death**. It appears to be linked with existing lung disease but whether this is due to heroin, adulterants, or other causes (e.g., cigarettes) is unclear.

Blood Clots

A thrombus is a blood clot. They form primarily in veins because blood moves more slowly in veins than in arteries. The clotting process is started by the platelets in the blood, which adhere to some surface. Normally, the walls of the veins are too smooth to allow this, but injection scars inside of veins create such surfaces. To reduce the risk of clotting; exercise and pay particular attention to the parts of your body in which you inject. These clots may stick in the walls and form hard clumps that interfere with the flow of blood. These are fairly common amongst injectors. They are usually frightening at first, but over time users find that they aren't particularly painful and that they don't seem to cause any problems other than making the vein in which they reside useless for injection.

High Blood Pressure

All of the garbage that gets introduced into the body as a result of the ingestion of un-pure heroin can cause many different problems. These foreign substances can react with each other and with normal parts of the body to produce particulate matter. Over time, this material will be removed from your body. But until then, it will often be found floating through your blood stream. The presence of this material constricts the flow of blood and so leads to high blood pressure. This situation is particularly bad for addicts. First, addicts do not stop using long enough for their bodies to recover and expel the foreign substances. Second, almost all addicts smoke cigarettes. Third, most addicts do not eat well; the number one junkie food is high in fat: pizza.

Infrequent chippers should not have to worry so much about high blood pressure. Regardless, all heroin users should check their blood pressures often, I recommend once a week.

Liver Damage

The liver may be infected due to viruses introduced in the administration process. Life is not possible without the liver. It is the primary means by which your body removes toxins. Many drugs are very straining to the liver; heroin is not. But unclean administration can introduce any number of viruses which can attack the liver.

Tetanus

Tetanus comes from the tetanus bacillus that lives in the intestines of all animals (including humans). It is excreted in fecal matter and can live in soil indefinitely. For obvious reasons it is most commonly found in manure. It lives in dead tissue (like skin) and does not cause local inflammation--this is one reason why it is such a dangerous disease; you often won't know that you have it until it is too late. The tetanus bacillus creates a toxin which it passes to the central nervous system. This toxin causes the nervous system to misbehave - telling muscles to stiffen and often causing painful spasms and convulsions. The first muscles affected are usually the jaws which explain why Tetanus is often referred to as "Lock Jaw." If the respirator muscles are affected, asphyxiation can occur. This point cannot be stressed enough: Tetanus from even a very small wound can kill you. Stay current on your Tetanus shots.

Watch Out: Most of the diseases that are of concern to heroin users have similar symptoms. These symptoms are listed in the table below. If you notice any of these, you should consult with a doctor. Most of the diseases are curable and those that are not can be helped greatly by a doctor.

Symptom
Long-term fever
Blood in urine
Paralysis
Abscesses
Petechiae
Difficulty Breathing
High Blood Pressure
Uncontrollable Muscle Tightness
Vomiting
Diarrhea
Weight Loss

9 - Awareness & Education

The S.A.F.E. project is about creating hope, awareness, and change surrounding the drug epidemic that we're facing in the United States.

I believe the best solution to the drug epidemic is awareness and education. When we are aware of something we know better and when we educate ourselves and others then we do better. Much of what people hear on the streets about drugs comes from those selling them. Recovery isn't a monthly thing, it's lifelong. We can't just depend on school programs to promote addiction awareness with our youth, we all need to educate ourselves and get involved because this is going on in your backyard. Doesn't matter what life style you are, you are affected. Education and awareness is HUGE. I'm a huge advocate for addiction awareness and it doesn't come from me being an addict because I've never been; it comes from me losing so many people to this epidemic. Starting The S.A.F.E. project is meant to give people hope, set awareness, educate them so they can educate others; not turn them away. You cannot give up and family and friends need to stick together. Help me set awareness and educate others on what is really going on. Between doctors, pharmaceutical companies and not enough in-house rehab places, I can only do so much. I need to get as many people involved as possible. Hold signs, tell your story, let people know we are here for them and let the dealers know we want them out of our towns. No more of our loved ones on memorial cards. If you're state offers Naloxone (Narcan) training, please get trained. It can reverse an overdose, for more details research online.

Let's not ignore the problem at large, let's do something about it. These people are NOT junkies, addicts as I use in this book or deadbeats, they have a real issue here and we need to help them. They are human beings and someone's son, daughter, grandchild and friend. It's not what we don't know now that will make a difference, it's what we do know and how we're going to move forward with getting these people help and having longer jail sentences for the dealers. Addicts don't need jail they need rehabilitation. Please check my blog for my book tour, Addiction Awareness Rally's and Circle Group Support Chats in your state towards spreading addiction awareness.

10 - Recovery & Detox

You can't predict the cards you're dealt and why some people or something's even happen in our lives. I believe everyone is here for a reason, to learn from them. Also, to take in the moments with them and death for me is how short life truly is and to remember the moments, not what took them away from us. Recovery is a process and unfortunately doesn't just happen, you have to work towards it and want it; you have to be willing to go through the awful process of detox for the recovery process to start. The word Im<u>possible</u> says <u>Possible</u> and I believe in possibility and that we all hold the key to capability of doing and having better in our life. The recovery process begins with you, I believe in you and now I need you to believe in yourself. I want to help you help yourself.

~ Corey Phinney

Realizing You Have a Problem

The very first step in *ANY RECOVERY PROCESS* is realizing you have a problem. It's very important that you realize a problem exists and that you need help overcoming it. Here are a few signs that you or someone you know is an addict:

- A sudden change in attitude and/or demeanor.

- Change of appearance or suddenly unconcerned with appearance.

- Fluctuation in weight

- Needle marks on arms, legs, hands, neck, or between toes

- Slow or slurred speech

- Do they have the shakes?

- Sweaty palms and/or cold and sweaty

- Dilated pupils (Like pins or real small)

- Presence of paraphernalia. (Needles, Baggies, Spoons)

Few heroin addicts have successfully recovered without some sort of professional help. I know a lot of people that couldn't do it without all of the support he or she was getting from family and friends. I really believe that realizing you're an addict is such an important first step. After that things start getting easier. You will know when you've hit rock bottom, if the things in your life are not what they once were. Example would be, not showing up to work, bills piling up, take off for a few days at a time. A lot of people do medical detox and/or rehabilitation; there are live in facilities and outpatient. There are so many ways of getting help, each state has free clinics; but some can cost thousands. Some health insurance companies even cancel out insurances to addicts if job changes, which then again sets the person back from getting the help that is needed. There are so many treatments out there, but finding the one that is right for you may be a little challenging but once you do, everything will fall back into place and you'll get control of your life back.

What is Detox?

Detoxification, in short detox, is the first move of the drug recovery treatment process. Withdrawal is the term used to describe the body's reaction to the removal of any substance it has come to be dependent on. Detox is the first step because until there is no alcohol or drugs in a person's body, withdrawal can cause severe craving for more. Additionally, while in a drug or alcohol induced state, a person is not fully prepared to participate in the educational and therapeutic process of rehab and treatment. Until the detox process is complete, someone is simply not ready for rehab, treatment and recovery. Withdrawal is caused by stopping or dramatically reducing drug use after heavy and prolonged use. The reaction frequently includes sweating, shaking, headache, drug craving, nausea, vomiting, abdominal cramping, diarrhea, inability to sleep, confusion, agitation, depression, anxiety, and other behavioral changes. Certain types of drugs require a period of medical detox; others do not. Opiates, such as heroin and methadone do require medical detox. Prescription medications, of all classifications, require medically supervised detox. Other illegal drugs, such as marijuana, crystal meth and cocaine (crack) do not require medical detox. Heroin withdrawal, being a form of morphine requires medically monitored detox. Heroin use causes a strong physical dependence and therefore withdrawal can result in serious complications. Heroin detox and withdrawal symptoms can include seizures, heart irregularities, vomiting, insomnia and the sweats. Once the body has adapted to the presence of the drug, withdrawal symptoms may occur if heroin use is reduced or stopped. Withdrawal, in regular abusers, may occur as early as a few hours after the last administration. It may also produce drug craving, restlessness, muscle and bone pain, diarrhea, cold flashes, goose bumps (cold turkey), leg kicking movements and various other physical symptoms. Most heroin detox and withdrawal symptoms peak between 48 and 72 hours after the last dose. Sudden heroin detox, withdrawal, by heavily users can be fatal. Several different schools of thought exist as to the best method for heroin detox. Medical heroin detox is done in a variety of ways including using methadone to taper, methadone maintenance or administering various drugs to prevent or minimize the physical side effects. Medical heroin detox always includes closely monitoring the person's vital signs (blood pressure and heart rate) for complications. Usually heroin detoxification takes four to seven days to complete the process.

11 - Finding Resources

There are a lot of resources online and all around you toward finding help and support groups. I recommend doing research and always ASK questions. If you're looking for yourself bring someone with you and don't be afraid to take the steps toward recovery. The S.A.F.E. project is great for online research, ask questions and join in on one of our online support group chats; we will even help you find a rehabilitation facility in your State. Do not get frustrated with the common insurance questions and delays and no beds available, that is sadly said across our country. Be positive and find the best program for you or your loved one. I have listed on page 57 and 58 some recommended sites to join that can help you with your research.

(All website links listed in my book ©2014 -**S.A.F.E.** has permission from each moderator)

12 - Emotions and Healing

The emotions and healing from a loss of a loved one to an overdose can cause so many emotions; there will be anger, could I have done more, the what if's, this is why we are here. This is the reason for this book and all we do, so you know that you are not alone. No one should see their loved ones on memorial cards due to addiction, and if I along with anyone else reading this could save just one person from addiction then I have done my job and I have done it well. After reading all the names that people shared with us in this book and sadly that's just a few; so many losses, so many young lives cut short. We will heal and we will not allow our loved ones to go un-noticed.

You will never forget the person you lost, but you will heal and it will all come in time. We must move on, not erase, but to share their stories and celebrate this person's life. You will feel all sorts of emotions; anger, sadness, remembrance, then trying to stay strong for all the people around you which is the easy part because you are passing your emotions off for another. You MUST heal before you can deal, so just let it all out. The healing process is a long road; we never truly heal our souls from losing the people we love, but we can educate others by telling our stories. Heal with keeping your loved one (s) alive through memories and pictures. You will find strength within you, maybe strength you didn't even know you had. You can only help someone when your soul is healed and only you will know when it is time. All we can do is make sure their name lives on forever. The name of the book is S.A.F.E., because everyone should feel and be SAFE. Allow yourself to go through the process of emotions and healing at your own pace. Join a local grievance group or talk to relatives and friends, just whatever you do, don't hold it in.

13 - Stress, Worrying, Anxiety

Letting GO is the hardest part. There may come a time during this process where you may just have to let them know they can no longer stay with you. Tough love, the feeling of not knowing where he or she will be staying; the stress, worrying, and anxiety will kick in. I had to part ways from my friends more than once, it was just too hard for me to watch them make bad choices and yes me to death that they were taking my advice and listening to me; when indeed they were just lying, using my car, I also enabled a couple of them because I believed they needed money for one thing and they used it for another. I felt hurt and used, but then I got smarter as I started learning more of how addiction works and I realized that this isn't my friend, this is the addiction. When my friends were wandering around the streets, it would give me anxiety not knowing where he or she was not knowing what they were doing; always waiting for the call I did not want to get – that my friend lost his or her battle to addiction. Addiction causes so much chaos in everyone's life. That is what addicts do not understand that it doesn't just affect them, it affects everyone involved. Addicts become great manipulators, especially at the beginning. Families and friends enable them and then once whoever it is giving them money catches on and shuts them off, they move on to someone else or even reverts to stealing once they run out of options. Anything can be a trigger. I know that people must want to help, but there is and wanting and sometimes help needs to be explained and forced upon so you do not enable them. Start with tough love and then support them on the road to recovery. Don't let the stress, worrying and anxiety get to you and soon as you find out that he or she is using, get help immediately. Don't let them talk you into something different, that they don't need help and so on. The earlier you get them into recovery, the better off you all will be.

14 - Addiction & Living Sober

If you are like me and didn't understand nor knew too much about addiction, then it starts with thinking like an addict. I lived in a day of my friend, seeing the streets he would go down to make a quick deal and how he would live his life without anyone knowing. I will always keep our conversations confidential, but it would sadden me to see what he did for money and how many people he hurt just for a fix. My friend always said he never felt loved and pretty much lost his soul to drugs and was trying so hard to refine who he was and find out what his purpose was in life. Everyone around him loved him. Even when he thought they didn't, they would always be the ones he would run to. I caught on quick and realized if I am going to help any of my friends beat this, I need to think like an addict and go through what they go through, without using of course. Listen to their stories and make mental notes of everything. *Knowledge is power,* when learning about addiction. I saw firsthand what an addict goes through when they go through withdrawals and how hard it is for them and everyone involved. To understand an addict, I feel you have to not become one, but ask the questions without judgment because you want them to trust you and you have to do it with an open heart and mind. I have learned more than I ever thought I would about addiction and I am happy I did. I will cherish the time I had with all of my friends who lost their battle with addiction and will work hard to educate and set awareness so no more lives will be lost.

Living Sober

Attend meetings at least three times per week and work on rebuilding trust with your family and re-connect with positive friends, while cutting out all the toxic people; only you know who is positive and who is toxic. Reach out to others in recovery. Remember you are responsible for your own sobriety, you can take advice and seek out support, but ultimately you need to be responsible for your own recovery. Exercising regularly is extremely important, it will help you feel better about yourself and also I recommend trying yoga, meditation, religion and self reflection; as these will help anxiety, possibility and your soul. Always do what works best for you, don't follow someone else's plan, do your own planning so you can be in control of your recovery. Never lie to yourself; if you feel you are, than you need to take an action of recourse and make some more changes. Don't keep things inside, forgive others; don't be bitter and as you forgive they will start their process of forgiveness as well. Keep a gratitude/life journal on all the things you are thankful for and all the things you want for yourself. Make a check list and check off as you accomplish. Do not get bogged down, start at the top of your list and work down, set a time frame on each goal. Do not feel sorry for yourself and remember tomorrow is the beginning of the rest of your life. Staying sober is hard enough so keep busy, especially in the first few months of sobriety. I understand alcohol may not be your problem, but try to have fun without it, trust me it is possible! Communicate with your family and close friends, communication is very important. Create a support network; get involved with AA or NA, any local groups and online support groups. Build an extended family of those who understand what you are going through. Take long walks, this helps clear your head. Take up a hobby; like painting, music, or writing to occupy the mind.

In your gratitude book write down 5 things you are thankful for each day; it can be anything from loving your family and friends to the air you breathe. Join an online recovery forum, it's only part of staying sober and who knows your story could help someone and you may even enjoy the discussions. Go back to school, educate yourself or take up a trade and improve your job skills to achieve your dreams. Reading and spending time with your family, you can really never do that enough. Make a bucket list and write down in your journal or on your calendar and then go out and do it! Travel, getting away really helps. If you don't have the financial means to go far then try camping or something within your budget, even a day trip of some sort. It is very important to not be around the same scenery; escape your comfort zone and try new experiences and challenges. Don't blame others, keep in mind that you are starting a new life and part of rebuilding is to let go. Do some volunteering in your community, this really helps re-build your spirits while meeting new adventurous people or get involved with a local recovery group(s). Always avoid one addiction for another, just because you are kicking one habit, don't replace it with gambling, drinking, or anything else. Stay focused on you and what you want to accomplish with your recovery. Never live in fear, accept that you can control some things and don't let the things you can't control, control you. If you do relapse, don't let it slip back into full out abuse. Accept that you are human and that you will slip up. Take massive action to make sure it doesn't happen again. You can control your recovery; just follow these steps while customizing your own plan that works for you. If you have any of your own tips on staying sober, please share on our social networking sites.

Remembrance

Below are just some of the names that families and friends have shared with me for the purpose of this book. I send much love to everyone who has lost someone to addiction. I will be re-doing an RV for my upcoming tour, so I will be posting on my personal blog if anyone would like to add names to this list I can add them; that is my gift to all of you and he or she will never be forgotten. Please see my blog for details.

Shaun Alan Flynn 10/7/77 – 9/28/12, John C. Homer 4/26/72 – 7/7/13 Bobby Dube 11/21/80 – 12/19/11, Marky Bleheen, Craig Daly 7/17/88 – 6/14/14, Paul BUPPA Canavan, Anthony Gilmore, Ronald Silva, Dennis Dillon, Nicole and Brian Shea, Jesse Todd Newcombe, Thomas Sniger, Julie Mather, Melissa Allen, Uncle "Tlti" 5/5/89, Daniel Thompson 11/10/1983-12/7/2013, Andy (Thomas) Anderson Jr., RW Nuttall, Michael Blonda, Robert Blonda Jr., Katie Johansen, Cory Hale 5/17/84 - 1/25/12, Derick Haward, Daniel Taylor, Salvatore Marchese, Joe Concepcion, Zach Paccitio, Paul Rogers, Robert Wilson, Sean Arnold, Allen Ferrell, John Lee Ferrell Anthony Buonopane, Brian Eldridge, Daniel Robert Silverman, Jesse A. Bolstridge, Frederick Turner, Julie Ricci, Joseph Ricci, Donald Bergeron, James Slattery, Michael Sparks, Stephen Pacheco, Dale Petersen, Monica Pellegrino, Kerri Lapham, Wayne Hardin, Walter Medina, Lords Watson, Adam Thomas. David Loubier, Jr 6/6/79-4/27/05. , Jason Keith, Ryan Donovan, Vick Fainer, James Flanagan, Colleen Libby, Adam Federico, John Daggett, Kara Ferris, Rhonda Zablocki, Mitchelle Driscoll, Michael McMahon, John Fraine, Richard Greene, Jessica Bauer, Liz Steal, Jason Gillis, Richie Emma 11/9/77 – 2/13/11, Heather Haegele, Joshua Weigand, Todd A Mount Jr, Gary Gibbons, Mic Talbert, Chelsea Angelina McCullough, Mandy ,Butler, Branden Deering 12/7/85 - 12/9/13, Kissendra Ritchey 12-20-12, Denny Bristow, Colleen Morgan, Patrick Velasco, Herman Gansert, Keith Meyer, Katrina Detty, Anthony "Tony" Paddock, Rodolfo Zaragoza Sr,

Kathy Napier, Jesse Anthony Bolstridge, Brandon Dawson, Bobby Glatfelter, Melissa Ann Sturm, Tony Hartlaub, Eric Breyan, Evan Greene, Nickolas Nusz, David S Marshall 2/8/2014, Matthew Tulloss 11/6/2012, Eric M Franklin, Robert M Franklin, Jesse Hoffman, Ricky Wiser, Eric Spry 7/21/2013, Ched Hudgins, Krystle, Scottie Mead, Paul Robinson, Thayer D. Stump Jr 10/12/94 - 02/08/13, Ronald Schroeder, Ryan Noel Bock 3/08/2014, Scott Simek, Eric Foster 11/26/86 - 01/08 / 13, Billy Souza, Tyler Keister, Donald Benware Jr, Kevin Wooddell, Megan Orange 8/16/94 – 8/19/13, Shannon M. Simmons 6/5/1983 - 05/20/2011, Samuel David Malter 11/1/11, Jamie Glenn, Sabrina Breitenbach 5/15/86-4/12/14, Tomothy Steil 1/24/1992 – 7/2/2011, Bryan Bihun 10/2/13, Tyler Thome 2/2/13, Johnny Honeycutt 2/2014, LeeAnne Patton, Samantha Lea Loomans, LeeAnne Evelyn Patton "Lucy", Jordan Harley 7/18/1987-5/13/2013, Ashley R. Barrett 11/6/1988 10/12 /2013, Tera JoAnn Guest 8-22-89 - 1-29-14, Charlie (Chuck) W Burk 12-13-74 - 12-22-1998, Erich Fritz 10/28/83 - 5/23/12, Ivana Wozniak, Graeme Andrew Johnson 7/10/84 – 8/8/13, Jason William Nolan 9/03/78 – 3/03/2011, Melanie Roush – Caruso, Ryan Shane Thompson 6/1688 – 12/28/12, William Wentz, Samantha Lauren 11-6-88 to 4-22-12, Eric Adam Obradovic 06/10/84-12/09/09, Corey Zinneman, Sherry Witters, Angel Hawley, William Anderson 7/21/64-3/5/09, Jacob Michael Paddy 2/21/90 - 7/19/13, Matthew Donald Delaney 7/17/84 – 7/30/13, Owen X. Kemp 1/12/1994--11/5/2013, Gregory T. Osmond Sr 02/22/68 - 09/16/13. , Shelby Perkins 11/12/89 - 05/21/10, Austin Dwyer, Leslie Marie Cathey 2/7/89 – 10/19/13, Lisa Coates Perry 1966 - 2010, Lonnie K. Overbee 5/22/67 – 6/27/10, Jordan Andrew Garling 2/17/89 – 3/11/11, Erik Hansen Coolbaugh 09/27/1979. 01/22/2009, Erin and Travis Edwards, Geraldine Korner, Jennifer Watts, Michael Robert "GAT" Godwin, Evan Lewis 10/5/90 – 3/20/14, Zachary Tyler Moe 5/27/91 – 8/3/2013,

Ryan Stadtfeld 10/15/84 – 9/6/12 , Mike Muelchi, Brittany Bovinett, Kennyth Catlin 11/7/64 – 11/1/09, Sean Yates 12/26/92 – 11/21/13, Kelsey Shane, Christina Marie Maldonado 7/1/92 - 2/8/14, Annette Dick 11/3/89- 3/27/14, Ryann Anderson, Lain Johnson 08/02/1977-11/12/12, Randy 'RED' Beaty Jr., Josh Pearlman , Derek Klingensmith, Joey Tipinski, Phillip "fooey" Frame, Steven Anthony Hundley 10/11/88 – 2/21/14, Harlin Pursley, Denny Maxon, Nate Ogles, Dustin Skinner 3/6/83 – 7/31/13, Rachel Elizabeth Grindal, Jody Lee Schaffer 10/14/79 – 11/10/10, Dwight D Adkins 3/10/57 – 10/1/09, Richard D Lutz 10/5/79 – 10/16/11, Mark Riedel 12/21/85-10/29/13, Sabra Scroggin 9/24/91 – 3/9/14, Adam Mackey 4/11/80-6/30/2006, Melissa Keeling 9/8/85 – 2/15/14, Anthony Gilmore 8/17/86-9/11/13, Bryan Austin Niemi 6/16/87 – 9/6/13, Martin Therit 12/8/78 - 04/6/13, Jessica Reedy, Andy Katchuk 10/10/88 - 2/11/11, Brandon Alcorn 11/22/88-7/28/12, Chad Moore 7/25/80-10/25/12, David Heath Clemons 5-23-81 - 1-1-13, Nicholas Thomas Specht 7/16/83 – 8/8/13, Keith Meyer, Mackenzie Danielle Freeze 6/8/1992 - 04/9/2013, Chet Thompson 2/8/86 - 8/19/2009, Tawni Pina 10/10/91 – 2/14/13, Zachary Duncan 04/01/1993 -05/04/14, Kyle Lapaolo 12/4/90 – 9/12/13, Jesse Todd Newcombe 8/3/93 – 9/15/13, Jacob Joseph Heider 9/21/87-2/19/14, Donald "Donnie" Ingram 10/13/66-08/05/13, Shaun O'Connor, Rose Jewell 10/05/71-02/10/07, Dustin Jewell 3/23/1990-02/11/2014, Autumn Cree Tryon 10/28/91 - 9/20/13, Garnett Hall, Jacob Dennis Schultz 10/30/89 - 11/5/11, Tarren Yuschak, Nicholas McKittrick 11/8/81-1/29/14, Benjamin "Ben" VanCamp 9/19/86 – 3/27/14, Kelsey Shane 2-8-90 -10-17-2013, Stacey Spegal, James J Smiley 3/31/65-8/28/2013, Larry Thompson, Johnathan Patrick Richards 03-31-1987-12-08-2007 , Michael S. Carte 1/6/85-6/24/09, William "Lee" Westmoreland Jr 2/1/90- 2/6/2012

Mike Finn 2/16/56 - 9/15/11, Cole Johns 9/8/1982-3/23/2014, Dan Nicolar, Michael Shawn Spencer 11/18/74 – 01/11/14, Benjamin John Oliphant 12/31/89 - 10/15/10, James Crook, Pamela Maybee, Denise Maybee, Chris Voiers 12-28-2010, Paul J McGregor 1/26/1982-4/18/2013, Robert Lee Keck 9/17/91- 3/10/14, Arthur "Artie" dunkelberger III 03/17/63 - 06/07/13, Callie Rough 9/18/71 - 3/18/14, Roy Raymond Cole III 06/06/79 - 09/18/2013, John Turntine, Judy Sheaper ,Amber Wills, Sandy & Joe wills, Chris Gamble, Steve Declue, Robey Morgan, Justin Blaine Meredith 05/23/1986 - 06/20/2009, Brandi Kaye Barnes 6/29/81-01/03/13, Channing Flores 9/25/85-8/26/12, Christina Lovelace, Joseph "Joey" Redmond Jr 2/5/80 - 10/20/10, Nick Sponsel 03/18/88- 10-17-2013, Scott Lincoln 5/21/70-12/10/01, Robert Boyer, Audrey-Rose Strother 3/11/1980 -11/26/2012, Donald Richard McGaha 9/6/80 – 4/11/14, Brittany Lynn Hefley 6/1/92 – 3/13/13, Kayla Susan Haubner 4/11/90 – 3/14/13, Ricky Wiser 2/9/79 - 8/24/2013, Mikel W. Jetter 11/11/80 – 12/27/13, Chad Moore 7/25/80 – 10/25/12, Amanda Willard 2/18/13, Annette Marie Dick 11/3/89 - 3/27/14, Krystal Day McGregor 8/30/92 - 4/18/13, Heather Lambert 7/22/91 – 10/17/14, My son, Derek Lee Sprouse 8/17/2013, Joe Taylor, Jacob Oeken 92-14, Valerie Bohn, Michael karol 9/18/1981 - 02/23/2008, Andrew Nicholas Holt 1/15/87 – 05/24/1994, Michael Kraus 1/12/12, Christopher Robert Dillon 7/4/94 – 11/18/13, Lucas Puterbaugh, James Allen Erickson 1/20/76 /08/01/14, Samantha M Franks 2/23/89-3/5/12, Shawn Martin Beatty, Melanie Bobel Wanner 4/29/14, Bridget Ford 10/20/2011, Nicole Swank 10/29/11, Danny Sain 8/25/13, Stephanie Hickman 1/12/14, Anthony Schmid 6/18/2012, Christopher Michael Clark 9/10/77 – 6/30/12, Valerie Anne, Erin and Travis Edwards. 2/7/2014, Nick Narez, Krista Byrd and Bobby Pogue, Joshua Ketcham, Richard Rosen, Joe Flan, Cherise Nelson 8/15/1982-3/28/2014, Erich Cole, Jared

Dudek, Melissa Ann Keeling, Sarah Britt 5/14/04, Matthew O. Kelley 06/03/2013, Jesse James, Ida Marie Naiper 10/2/12, Johnny Borczak, Randall Mayer 07/11/89 03/25/14, Nicole Kohler 11/23/79 5/29/2010, Brittany Danielle Drouillard 5/7/90-3/14/14, Brittany "LaGuera" Wilson, Kayla Meagan Perry. 9/16/94 9/24/13, Crystal Lynn Jolley 5/22/12, Jason D. Farmer 6/12/11, Russell Hudek jr 7/8/09, Daniel J.Niehorster 7/7/87-2/11/14, Tiffany Steel 11/6/11, Chelsea Rene Sands 12/25/13, Joshua Shank 07/12/90 02/19/12, Maryann Whitehead 4/22/1992 – 4/5/2014, Donald R McGaha 9/6 /1980 – 4/11/ 2014, Bryan d Hunter, George Lanza 3/1977 - 2/2013, Brittney Miller 1/26/86 - 3/13/14, Sean Michael Podolske, Arthur Vargas, Goche, Amber Richard 5/6/88- 8/ 15/ 10, Preston Brent Craig 7/16/78-3/11/06, Hank Kasavich 3/7/80 -12/10/11, Brandon Smith 8/12/92 - 3/14/14, Jason Straw 2/16/2014, Andrew Whalen 9/23/90-10/12/13, Andrew C. Miller 10/15/81-9/5/13, Ashley Barrett 10/12/13, Kelsey Fortner 8/6/88 - 12/29/13, Jamie Fields, Jordan Andrew Garling 02/17/89-03/11/11, Margaret and Abby Roe, Sandy Johnson 2010, Joshua Hart 5/13/79-1/25/11, Tiffany Harding 10-20-93 / 4-1-13. Jason Glover, Nick R. Winchenbach, Monica Ridgely, Elizabeth Stelle (penny), Doug Rollins, Carl Crawford 6/4/81-10/16/13, Tommy Gouveia 10/13/82 – 3/29/14, . Chad E. Moore 7/25/80-10/25/12, Nicole Kohler 1979- 2010, Tawni Pina 10/10/91 to 2/14/13, Nicole Ranalletta 3/30/95-12/14/13, Taylor Walters 06/30/1992- 02/26/2013, Chris 6/30/12, Zach Jungwirth, Joseph Brutcher and Tyler Brummett, Timothy Mullins 1/24/86 – 3/11/13, Sabra Scroggin 9/24/91 to 3/9/14, Kelsey Fortner 8/6/1988-12/28/2013, John Peters, Shane Cullen 21 years old, Ched Hudgins aka Cheddar, Michael Ostrowski, Mindi Richardson 11/25/73 – 12/6/12, Jessica Schultz, Samantha Lauren, Kathleen "Katie" Murphy, Graeme johnson, Brian Muns 7/2/76 – 8/30/12, Brad Goodin, Ashley Nicole Vaughn 10/20/85 – 01/27/07, Edward Kenneth Dillon III 1/06/81-2/04/12, Courtney Lynn. 3/6/85 – 3/2/10, Paul Andrew Fitzgerald 5/10/84 – 10/2/06

Strength & Recovery

John Roderick, Kirt Buckler, Lori Smallwood, Nicole Emminger, Mike Brissette, Amber Lea, Brandon Guyant, Kelli Riddell, Lacey Craig, Alissa Hanel, Brendan S Anderson, Anna Vigfusson, Christopher Reimer, Krista Amico, Earl Young, Jr., Krystal Miller, Brenda Whisenant, Alyssa Pahl Sober Since 5/31/12, Brittany Douglas, Laura Kohler, Amber Salter, Carissa Beck, Zachariah Masimore, Amanda Masimore, Britani Landis, Mary Thomas,William Andrews, Stephen Ashman, Rodney & Brooke Osborne, Mike Duggan, Keith Laporta, Matt Ganem, Steven Langley, Lisa Murray, Michele Maniscalco . Danny Sherburne. Mike Homer, Rich Melchionno, Joselito "Pito" Franquiz, Michael Maclaughlin. Ron Ward, Larry Moore, William Baker, Rick Rosenhagen, Steven Burke. Josh Davis. Derek Neressian.

If your name isn't listed, it doesn't mean you are not recognized because all who are in sobriety, from the bottom of my heart, I along with everyone from The S.A.F.E. project honor you! If you are in recovery and would like your name on the RV please check my personal blog for details.

The S.A.F.E. project's Affiliated Sites

*Fan Page: www.facebook.com/TheSAFEproject77

*Group: www.facebook.com/groups/TheSAFEproject

*www.twitter.com/TheSAFE_project

www.facebook.com/groups/SupportGroupChat/

www.facebook.com/NationalAddictionAwarenessRallyandMemorial

www.facebook.com/groups/VIGILandRECOVERY/

www.facebook.com/youthaddicted

Email: TheSAFEproject77@yahoo.com

Personal Sites & HashTags

www.coreyphinney77.blogspot.com
www.facebook.com/groups/CoreyJPhinney
www.facebook.com/CoreyJPhinney
www.twitter.com/coreyphinney
www.blogtalkradio.com/thesafeproject
www.youtube.com/user/coreyphinney
www.instagram.com/corespire
www.pinterest.com/coreyphinney

#TheSAFEproject / #CoreSpire / #AuthorCoreyPhinney

Recommended Sites to join

Wicked Sober offers free drug rehab assessment and placement through personalized assistance to those suffering from addiction as they begin their journey into recovery and a brand new life.
https://www.facebook.com/WickedSober

Though we are located in Northern Kentucky & Cincinnati we strive to help everyone in the world with the disease of heroin. We post news stories, videos, personal addiction stories and more each and every day. If you LIKE our page you will get our daily updates delivered straight to your news feeds in Facebook.
Latest heroin news, videos and personal stories.
https://www.facebook.com/heroinkillsyou

The objective of the coalition is to prevent opiate overdoses, prevent deaths from those who have overdosed, provide support and linkages to those who are using opiates, as well as their loved ones, and to create awareness about opioid overdose prevention.
https://www.facebook.com/pages/Brockton-Mayors-Opioid-Overdose-Prevention-Coalition/358161637624895

Rally photos & videos from Missouri, Illinois & any other states that would like to post their photo albums on this page. Please feel free to share any of your media to the page.
https://www.facebook.com/AntiHeroinRallyPhotosVideos

The Stairway To Recovery Center is a supportive beacon of light within the recovery community of Massachusetts' South Shore. The center is a place that promotes and exemplifies hope for recovering addicts; where peers are engaged in many aspects of recovery to gain the resources, skills and practical knowledge necessary to improve their quality of life.
https://www.facebook.com/Stairway2Recovery

Private group for heroin support **https://www.facebook.com/groups/heroinsupport/**
Post pictures and stories of loved ones lost to heroin.
https://www.facebook.com/LostToHeroin
Private group for loved ones lost to heroin.
https://www.facebook.com/groups/LostToHeroin

(All sites listed above, Author © Corey Phinney has permission from each moderator for publication of the book S.A.F.E.)

The S.A.F.E. project Pledge

I pledge not to use drugs and to help anyone who is as long as he or she is ready and willing to be helped. I pledge to promote Addiction Awareness anyway I can within my community and to be thankful for all of the blessings I've been given and to live my life to the fullest. I will live a positive life and will follow my dreams.

I_____ take The S.A.F.E. project Pledge on _____/_____/_____. That I will not let anyone stand in the way of my dreams and I WILL live a more fulfilled life. I will say NO to DRUGS and educate others on what I know to the best of my knowledge. I pledge to spread Addiction Awareness. By signing below you have taken The S.A.F.E. project Pledge.

Signature: _____

In Memory of:_____

In Strength of:_____

You can dedicate this page to someone or even to yourself!

I Dedicate this page to:_____

What are you MOST Thankful for?

_____
_____
_____
_____

List a few things you want in your Life?

_____
_____
_____
_____

List a few things you want out of your Life?

_____
_____
_____
_____

Where do you want to see yourself a year from now?

_____
_____
_____
_____
_____

Take a risk, do something you would normally not do and free yourself of fear and post on our Facebook Page what you did and how it made you feel.

Journal

(Take a few moments and write down your thoughts, write down anything. I believe in journals and that they solve problems and it's a wonderful tool to just write down how you feel.) I recommend purchasing a journal for everyday use.

I BELIEVE IN YOU

Special Thanks
"Together we WILL make a Difference"

I have so many people to be thankful for and if you're not noted in my book, you definitely are in my heart. I am so thankful and grateful for each and every person in my life and so thankful to be able to pay it forward toward helping others, it truly is my gift and my strength comes from within each person and each story I hear and it's you who does the real work, all I do is supply the platform for your voice to be heard. I thank all of my readers, followers and everyone who has stood by and believed in me as much as I believed in each one of you. I've always known my gift in life was to help others, but honestly I couldn't do it without all of the support, I truly love you all.
~ Corey phinney

John Phinney
Christine Ahern
Sherri Westhaver
Heather Kennedy
Nancy Leedberg
Colleen Roderick
Francis Sampson
Matthew Ganem
Mike Duggan
Keithy Laporta
Brandi-Jo MacLaughin
Danny Sherburne
Nicole Penticost
Jaden Westhaver

Shaun's Mom: Dottie Melchionno & Dad: AL Flynn and all of Shaun's Brothers, Sisters, Family and Friends.

My Dad: Billy Dwyer & Mom: Peggy Sarno –Solari. My Sisters, Loni, Courtney, Heather, and Amber Dwyer and my Beautiful Niece Mariah Dwyer, My Papa Edward Sarno and the rest of my Family and Friends, I love you!

I've always wanted children listed below, these kids are like my own and I treat them as if they where and each one gives me strength, love and grey hair lol.

Kyle, Dalton, Emmy & Mason Roderick

Thank you to everyone who purchased my book and this is just one way you can help me help others. Check my blog for T-shirts, Wristbands and Book ~ Corey

Please watch for my next book coming out *"The Grass isn't always Greener on the other side"*. Coming out in 2015 ~ Go on my blog for Book Tour Information and my around the U.S.A. Addiction Awareness Rally's, Volunteering and Circle Groups.

Made in the USA
Middletown, DE
03 February 2015